ANXIETY DISORDER
Handbook

ANXIETY DISORDER

Handbook

Third Edition

*A self-help approach
to treating anxiety and panic*

Jeffrey A. Roosa, LCSW-R

To order additional copies of this book, contact:
Jeffrey A. Roosa, LCSWR
P.O. Box 758
Middletown, NY 10940
39684

The

Anxiety Disorder Handbook

was developed through work with sufferers of

Panic Disorder
Agoraphobia
Post-traumatic Stress Disorder
Generalized Anxiety Disorder
Social Anxiety Disorder
Phobias
Obsessive Compulsive Disorder
ADHD and ADD
Eating Disorders
Bipolar Disorder
Separation Anxiety Disorder
Asperger Syndrome
and more

This handbook was made possible
through the loving support of my
wife Lynn,
and by the
love of my children.

When I dedicated my practice in the field to anxiety disorders in 1998, I did so because I saw many people suffering without any clear-cut approach for treatment. The self-help options at the time seemed more like reading the tabloids, without any significant solutions; and the medical community had their cure, antidepressants, which themselves had awful side effects that reportedly stripped away more of the user's dignity if you got those (the side effects).

My goal was clear, to set out in search of things that actually worked for people with anxiety and panic. Here is what I found:

Panic disorder, generalized anxiety disorder, post-traumatic stress disorder, social anxiety disorder, separation anxiety disorder, and the phobias are significant forces in the lives of those people who suffer from these conditions. Anxiety disorders are disorienting, frustrating, and frequently make the sufferer feel like he/she is going crazy.

Adults who suffer from an anxiety disorder often have the condition first diagnosed by a family physician, who often times offer their patients a drug to combat the problem. However, many people find out down the road that this remedy falls short in stopping the problem and for a good reason. It is merely a Band-Aid approach to treatment. The drug covers up some of the symptoms, but it does not treat the problem. Oftentimes the sufferer continues to feel the effects of his/her anxiety, even under treatment with medication, on some levels. If not immediately, shortly down the road, many find that the symptoms which sent them to the doctor in the first place will again resurface.

Children who suffer from anxiety disorders are often brought to their pediatrician by their parents when the symptoms become problematic. Some of these children are referred to a behavioral specialist for treatment, and that's great! However, many are misdiagnosed as having ADHD and are placed on medications for that disorder. There are significant parallels between anxiety and ADHD/ADD; but for whatever reason, many doctors see ADHD/ADD more when they look at child behavioral problems more than anxiety.

It has become my understanding that the problem itself must be addressed in order to relieve the symptoms of an anxiety sufferer. To do this, we must first dissect the condition itself, and the fear from which most of the anxiety conditions originate.

FEAR

Let's face it; everyone has experienced fear at one time or another—no one is immune! Factors such as where we live, work, and so forth have a bearing on what degree of danger people are used to experiencing. An electrician working with high voltage electricity while suspended on a ladder certainly faces more substantial danger than does a telemarketer. Yet a telemarketer living in Philadelphia may experience more danger than one living in semirural Pine Bush, New York. Using the parameters set in the example given: When the electrician experiences fear, it is directly related to dangers that exist in his work environment. This reaction would be viewed as common and appropriate. Likewise, the telemarketer living in Philadelphia may feel his heart rate jump after an encounter with a rage-filled commuter on his way to work. Fear that is experienced in direct connection to a real danger is the normative fear and anxiety that everyone experiences from time to time.

PANIC ATTACKS

Panic attacks exceed normal fear and anxiety because they occur while no specific danger or object threatens the individual. The person is just suddenly overwhelmed with brief attacks of anxiety, apprehension, and then terror. These people experience an exaggerated version of the common and adaptive fear that each of us has felt on many occasions.

The American Psychiatric Association (2000) states that four or more of the following symptoms occurring abruptly and reaching a peak within ten minutes indicates a panic attack.

- Palpitations, pounding heart, or accelerated heart rate.
- Sweating
- Trembling or shaking
- Sensations of shortness of breath or smothering
- Feeling of choking
- Chest pain or discomfort
- Nausea or abdominal distress
- Feeling dizzy, unsteady, lightheaded, or faint

- Derealization (feeling of unreality) or depersonalization (being detached from oneself)
- Fear of losing control or going crazy
- Fear of dying
- Paresthesias (numbness or tingling sensations)
- Chills or hot flushes

You must experience four or more of the preceding symptoms for your situation to be classified as a panic attack. If not, you are experiencing panic features, but you are not experiencing the full attack. A little bit of a bad thing is still a bad thing! Sufferers of panic features are also experiencing a high degree of anxiety and can also be helped by this handbook. When clients go through a panic attack, they often feel paralyzed and terrorized by the experience.

Panic Attacks End

Sufferers must come to terms with an essential feature of panic attacks—that they end! The entire attack typically lasts from seconds to several minutes, and then the symptoms go away. While people initially see little comfort in this information, they come to realize through repeated exposure to this idea that it is truly valuable. Let's make that step 1. Write it down! Say it to yourself five or six times a day until it's internalized. Understanding that attacks do have a beginning and an end is crucial because fearing future attacks is common among panic sufferers. It certainly takes away a degree of their *power (which we will touch on later).*

You Are Not Alone

Whenever stress or tragedy happens to people, their immediate response is to see the personal cost. Step 2 is coming to an understanding that many people suffer from panic attacks—that you are not alone! This is important information to a panic sufferer, who sometimes may feel like they will go crazy, or lose control. Additionally, it changes the perspective of the disorder from a personal suffering to a community suffering. This benefits the panic sufferer, who often experiences low self-esteem as part of the disorder. Write this down. Say it to yourself five or six times a day until it becomes part of the way you think about the problem. You must reintroduce this idea regularly so that you learn to appreciate the idea that you are not alone. Often, when experiencing a panic attack, clients feel isolated from the rest of their world. By understanding your connection to others on a regular basis, you can internalize the thought and diminish the irrational belief of isolation. I call this process of changing thought patterns, cognitive restructuring; and this is the main clinical effort in treating panic, or any anxiety disorder. Cognitive restructuring changes irrational thought patterns to rational ones, which in turn greatly diminishes panic symptoms.

Case # 1

Dawn is a twenty-six-year-old single mother, who works as a secretary. She was sexually abused by a neighbor at the age of five, and again by a cousin at the age of nine. She never told anyone about these past assaults. Lately, she has realized that she has a constant flood of thoughts about all the things going on in her life. She finds it difficult to get to sleep at night; and when she does get to sleep on time, she finds that she wakes up in the middle and cannot go back to sleep. She has had a series of unexpected panic attacks at work, and while driving. She states that she is being worn down by the combination of these stressors. She is finding it difficult to concentrate at work.

Illogical Thoughts

To say that a person has irrational or illogical thought patterns does not imply "crazy" or psychotic thought. In this case, it is important to consider the origins of these thought patterns, which are often linked to some original stressor in the client's past. In Dawn's case, the sexual abuse that she suffered as a child. Sometimes, the original stressor may be immediately apparent, such as in the case of early childhood abuse (sexual, physical, or emotional); but many times the original stressor is extremely personalized and difficult to pinpoint. Either way, you should not put too much emphasis on the original stressor because, while you may acknowledge the event, this may hold little connective value to your emotions attached to it. People repress things, shoving them deep into the unconscious, to avoid feelings that the conscious mind cannot handle. The clinical significance here is that when the original stressor occurred, the individual had no frame of reference with which to process it. Human beings require life's events to hold a degree of predictability, without which, it would be difficult to maintain our sanity (Peter Marris 1975). So when the original stressor occurred, the person filed it in a mental framework that he/she could understand, distorting the facts and truths about the situation that he/she could not have known with his/her limited frame of reference. It is here where illogical/irrational thoughts are born.

For example, Dawn had never been sexually abused prior to age five. She had never discussed the topic, nor had she overheard anyone discussing it. The experience must have been like seeing an alien. She had no prior experience from which to draw on, emotionally, physically, or in any other way. Dawn made up a rationale for the abuse that helped her survive the experience—an irrational thought. Over her lifetime, she had to use the logic that developed that day repeatedly; and she gradually learned that it was an illogical hypothesis. As the rationale for the experience broke down overtime, her stress grew. During the original stressor, Dawn most likely took in her surroundings and simultaneously sought a rationale for what was happening. In searching for a rationale, her mode of thinking would come into play. At that age, individuals utilize magical thinking to a great degree. In using the thought patterns at her disposal to make heads or tails of a more complex, adult emotional situation, she did not process the original stressor as an adult would because she had no frame of reference. The way she did process the event is probably a distorted one, but it worked for her at the time! When something works, we tend to stick with it. It won't be until years later, when the outside world gives her information to challenge her thoughts about the event, that she will even consider the event again—most likely on an unconscious level. The contradictions will overwhelm her, as those illogical/irrational beliefs had been built upon for years. Her self-identity and self-esteem are suddenly threatened; and the girl, now a woman, tries to deny the event(s) as it begins to resurface. However, in a world full of talk shows and magazines, that's a difficult thing to do. The woman finds it easier to disprove the idea that her thoughts are flawed by becoming involved in an adult relationship with someone like the abuser, and proving that she can make it work. Often this line of thinking has tragic results.

Buried Feelings

Despite realizing the original stressor, no one should ever purposely work toward uncovering buried feelings. They will uncover themselves overtime spent in therapy, and premature revelations could be damaging. Remember, people repress thoughts that they cannot emotionally deal with, and uncovering such before you are prepared to handle it is negligent at best! This is why I feel that hypnosis is dangerous to people with true unrecalled memories.

Overcontrol

When a person internally decides that they have trouble dealing with new situations, what do they do? They try to overcontrol their surroundings! Do you know anyone like that? Of course, you do! This is called anxiety building. The person seeks predictability in his/her world; but because of their anxiety, they find little relief, only frustration. This causes a more intense course of environmental control, building more anxiety.

This constant effort of thought becomes quite troubling to the client, who even finds it difficult to go or stay asleep with the constant cognitive effort. One of my clients once referred to this as "waiting for the committee to settle down." This statement is different than psychotic thought patterns, as that client is well oriented to people, places, and things around them. Nevertheless, it is a troubling predicament to the client, who seeks relief.

Flood of Thoughts

People who suffer from anxiety disorders commonly experience this flood of thought, which is troubling to them and lacks any adaptive value. The dilemma is that most sufferers believe that there is value in the many thoughts that race through their minds, which is their reason for allowing the process to occur in the first place. They often report the need to solve life's problems in this way, although they never succeed. Sufferers lose sleep because of the constant thinking and generally express frustration in their lack of control. Sufferers have also reported a degree of paranoia, as their constant thought about people in situations reportedly created thoughts of false jealousy, false betrayal, false emergency, and more. All of them required the sufferer to ponder those situations even further, thus bringing up real feelings of anger, etc. Many of my clients find these events "ruin" their lives as neither they, nor the people around them, understand the events—leading to misunderstandings. This happens to the school-aged child as often as the adult!

Permission to Rest

One must first acknowledge that the flood of thoughts is not good for them, that sleep is essential to their survival. They must give themselves permission to be at rest. This is an extremely difficult task to the sufferer, as they see their attention to their thoughts as essential to their survival.

Focusing

Immediate relief is available from the constant flow of thought associated with anxiety through focusing techniques. The sufferer's inability to focus is what enables their minds to run unchecked.

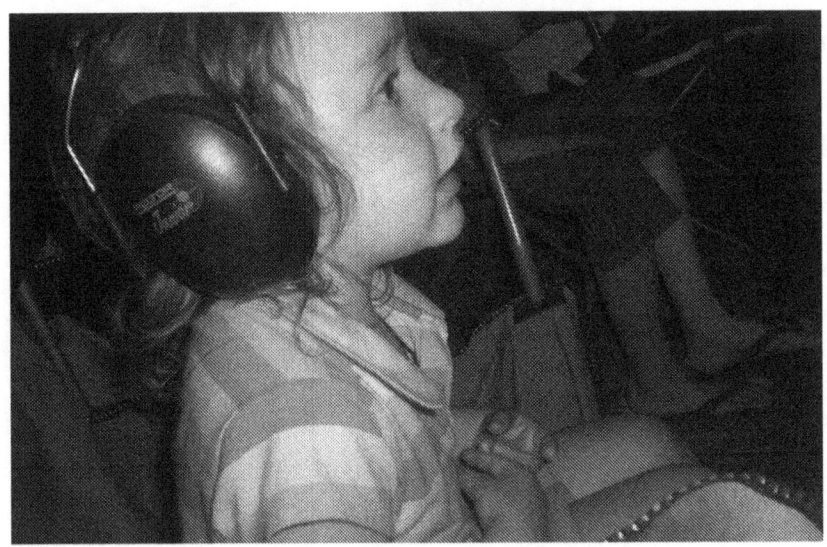

Focusing Technique

After you have gotten it into your head that

1) Panic attacks end.
2) You are not alone in suffering from panic attacks.
3) You accept that you have some irrational thought patterns that underlie your condition.

Then you are ready to learn focusing techniques. Focusing techniques are meaningless if they are not practiced and internalized. They may even seem a little silly at first, but you will wonder how you lived without them after you use them for a while. The most basic technique that I tell my clients to utilize is *saying the alphabet backward* in times of racing thoughts. The idea of this technique is often intriguing to the client, as it promotes looking at something familiar in a different way. The familiarity of the alphabet allows for a certain comfort level. While this technique proves effective initially, many clients soon memorize the effort, rendering it useless. That's okay because the relief it gives the client for a period of time proves to the person that they can overcome the symptoms of their suffering! Often a client will tell me that it "doesn't work" for them, and I soon realize that the client is caught up in their success or failure in the task. It should be noted that the intended purpose is in doing the task itself, which produces focusing. This is the client's anxiety at work, pushing them to be the best they can be. So do not worry if this task is difficult for you—it's supposed to be! Just do it!

One of the second focusing techniques that I use with my clients involves a U.S. penny. That's right! *A penny*. Upon introducing the technique, I give the client a penny and tell them to hold it between their thumb and index finger, with Lincoln's head under their thumb. This is like an anxiety litmus test, as the client frequently overexamines the penny with multisenses, as opposed to merely just feeling it, searching for the secret or something. This is an indication of how anxiety sufferers flood themselves with sensory information. This is clearly one of those situations where too much information is not a good thing.

Do you overstimulate yourself? Pay attention to how you examine things, and you will be able to tell. This is a very basic means to show you how evident your anxiety actually has become. It further gives you a clear picture of the anxious process in action, which many of my clients find startling.

> It really works. You never know how much the anxiety is affecting you until the traffic slows down.
>
> —former client

Anxiety or panic sufferers appear to never have the time to dissect their thought patterns because there are too many thoughts being attended to at any given time. They only know that these thought patterns are disturbing to them. Imagine—all of this insight from a mere penny! So let's try it! Now, just use your sense of touch. Try closing your eyes, if that helps. Develop a mental picture of Lincoln's head by rubbing the penny. Can you feel Lincoln's head? The date of the penny? The words on the penny? The shape of the penny? How is it working? Are you able to get the mental picture of Lincoln's head? You will have to try it several times before you get it in that noggin, but you will eventually succeed if you keep trying. Many people will not understand why they are instructed to do this exercise in the first place; but if you are committed, you will begin to see the benefits. People must have a very high level of commitment to work on panic or anxiety, because *it is work,* and it is frustrating. You have to believe that you can beat it! It will be quite a relief to take control of your thoughts again! I usually tell clients to practice this focusing technique five to six times daily for best results.

Why a Penny?

The use of the penny came about in searching for an item that could be transported by the client yet was common in our society and held no associative value.

Eventually you will internalize the picture of the penny itself; and you will naturally, and without thinking about it, use this technique when your mind becomes flooded with thought. You will have incorporated it into your way of handling the problem. When my clients look at me in disbelief when I suggest that this be possible, I remind them of a time when they could not succeed at tying their shoes. They recalled how many times they practiced until they got it right, and how they no longer put much conscious thought into the action today at all! It's pretty much the same for driving a car! Think about it. There are many things that you can eventually use to focus on, but be careful on what items you choose. Many people often tell me that they focus on other individuals when their minds become flooded with thought. The flaw in using another human being is that we attach emotions to our relationships with others. So while you may be thinking about your girlfriend, wife, or child, there are many other feelings and experiences produced that add to your stress level.

Case # 2

Greg is a twenty-two-year-old single college student who is struggling with panic attacks and obsessive-compulsive behavior features. He disclosed during a therapy session that he uses his girlfriend to focus on, but that it rarely works for him.

In the example above, Greg's attempt at focusing failed because he doesn't always get along with his girlfriend. Sometimes he does, sometimes he doesn't; and he rarely thinks of her without attaching emotional content. So the penny does just the trick! Just don't tell Greg's girlfriend!

Once you have developed your focusing abilities, it is time to move on to relaxation techniques. But you cannot discuss relaxation without discussing the comfort zone.

Comfort Zone

The comfort zone is a place in which a person suffering from panic feels comfortable. There are great differences from person to person as to their comfort zones. As a matter of fact, it is easier for clients to tell me the places in which they are uncomfortable. For some it's the supermarket, for others it's driving on a highway. For some sufferers, they may have few, if any, places in which they feel completely comfortable. When the client feels that they have breeched the boundaries of this space, a panic attack or significant anxiety often occurs. The previously mentioned focusing techniques help the client develop a comfort zone within them, one which they can take with them wherever they go! But focusing alone does not always do the trick!

Guided Imagery

Guided imagery is used in two ways to assist in the treatment of anxiety. The first way would be as a form of exposure therapy, even though the client never leaves the comfort of their chair in the therapist's room. Here's how it works: (1) The client is asked to close their eyes. (2) Then, for example, to picture a large ship sailing on the ocean. Go ahead try it! Picture yourself standing on the deck at the back of that large ship. Suddenly, the scene turns into a cartoon. You look to your side, and Popeye is standing next to you. Popeye picks up a large chain with an anchor on the end of it. He swings the anchor around and around and then tosses it into the ocean. *Ker-plop!* What happens to the boat? I often get a variety of answers to this question that let me know how far the client has progressed in treatment thus far, what issues still need to be worked on, and the client's current commitment to the work. Most clients report that the ship comes to a stop. (However, I do hear sometimes that the anchor's submerging causes it to pull in the ship, or any of many variations.) I then ask them: open your eyes and look around. What do they see? Most report that they see gentle waves, maybe a bird. What do they hear? The sound of the waves hitting/patting the boat is a common response (although some people start using the Popeye voice). I then ask them to take a deep breath. What do they smell? They often say that they smell the pleasant salty sea air. How do they feel? *Relaxed*. I then tell the client that they can go to their ship whenever they experience stress. The technique is of a higher level because it utilizes imagination, factual occurrence, and concentration (the three levels of cognition: magical, concrete, and abstract) (Kaplan 1980). In this way, I can measure where a client's thoughts are predominant, and it aids the clinician in focusing treatment efforts. The technique permits the client to transcend a bad situation, one in which they feel out of control, to state relaxation; however, the client must be doing the work to reach the point in which this technique can be beneficial. For it to be used as a tool, they must first have had mastered focusing. Sometimes the situation of being on a ship in the ocean is a phobia itself, requiring a degree of work in that direction or altering the technique to a horse in a meadow. The clinician uses whatever works for the client.

Exposure Therapy

At this point in treatment, the client has been well armed with tools to combat panic attacks and their anxiety, but practicing those has been situational at best because of the unpredictable nature of the problem. Exposure to stressful situations aids the client in utilizing focusing techniques at proper times and intervals. It is the clinician's job to determine the degree to which the client can handle exposure to stressful situations. It would be irresponsible on the part of the clinician to expose a client to situations that would be too stressful, and yet the point of exercise is for the client to experience some stress. How is this stress level determined? By asking! Some clients are so fearful of certain situations that merely the thought of those anxiety-provoking moments is enough for the full experience. For example, a snake phobia sufferer is often quivering of the mere mention of the animal. For these clients, we take mental trips, in which the client is exposed to snakes. To begin with, I usually ask the client about their earliest memory of seeing a snake and let them tell their story. All the while I am looking for associations, a mental link that people sometimes develop when two or more situations occur simultaneously. Exposure to one often arouses feelings of the other(s). Like when you listen to a particular song from your past. Anyway, the client completes their first contact story, and I support the client. It is common for the first snake contact to be a surprise followed by a feeling of being scared. Most people would respond the way the client did in that situation, and it is important that the client realize this with the remaining portion of the session; if there is time, I would use guided imagery to return to that moment of first contact and to explore the client's feelings.

The client often reports the horror of the surprise, and I ask why aren't you pleased with being surprised at the party?

With a gift from someone special? The client frequently looks bewildered, becomes a little frustrated, and says "But it's a snake!" I reply, "That's right; it's a snake (leaving silence for momentary thought)." The client often says, "It could have bit me. It may have been poisonous!" I reply, "Oh, you are playing the 'what if' game; I didn't realize that. Next time you have to let me know in advance. Anyway, time is up. I will see you next week when we can play some more." The client leaves frustrated, but thinking. The point of the exercise is to attack the fearful flow of thought by pointing it out to the client who has incorporated the process into his/her being without question. We would continue using guided imagery until the client is prepared to visit the local pet store during session, or the places that he/she believes they will encounter a snake. The object of the therapy is, of course, to desensitize the client to the snake with repeated therapeutic exposure. The client finds it easier to confront his/her fears with the therapist there. It is very effective. I often remind clients to breathe, focus, or to go to their special place (the ship, etc.) during these exposures when they report fear; it makes therapy move rapidly.

Client Empowerment in the Therapy

The clinician can then ask the client about other useful items that he/she can think of as focusing centerpieces.

Most often the client chooses some other person or event. Can you figure out why either of these would be poor choices? Because both people and events are often emotion laden and bring with them many additional thoughts, people, and emotions to consider. Remember, we are trying to curb runaway thought patterns, not set them in motion. After carefully explaining this to the client, the clinician should offer some good suggestions. As panic attacks often occur while the client is driving, an interesting key chain to play with can be a good focusing tool! If you bought it for this purpose, it might even be slightly humorous! Smiling and laughter are strong motivators to all!

Owning and possessing a cell phone while driving sometimes breaks the thoughts of isolation that help foster panic attacks in the car. Knowing that you can literally reach out and call someone can be quite comforting. I often tell my clients to tape phone numbers to the car's dashboard of people who may be available to receive a call during particular drives. This also can have an impact on irrational thoughts of impending doom, because the ability to confirm is present without having to begin checking behaviors. It is the clinician's job to reinforce this idea in the client so that they internalize their ability to conform. This is a difficult task for the clinician. Especially with OCD clients, but a necessary one!

As previously stated, the clinician must explore and find items for focus from the clients' own examples. This makes the focusing exercise that much more familiar and personal. It also increases the ability of the technique to work quickly.

Blaming and Displacement

Often clients come to me and, upon initial disclosure, tell me that their partners in their adult relationships are causing the problems in some way. These particular clients seem to understand their own dysfunctional early-life relationships, and that of their own partner; but they do not see the connection to their present life problems. They don't understand why they have panic attacks and anxiety. I often tell these clients to stop looking for a connection, as that type of work brings no immediate satisfaction—it's timely and frustrating. This brings up the concept: "The past is the past." Now this is an essential concept in life because it gives us true emotional perspective. Why invest emotions on events or situations that no longer exist? Many people do this, and it appears to be just another example of giving away one's power.

Getting back to the client now, I ask them what is the one similar element between their past and present (and possibly future). I have the clients ponder over this for many sessions. The client often gets angry and frustrated, stating that they came to me for the answers. I follow by saying that I believe they enter the therapeutic relationship with their answers, but that their minds are too clouded to see them. That it is not for me to point the answers out even if they are readily apparent because then the client would have learned nothing. I see my role as providing structure for the therapeutic process to take place. In this manner, the client learns the answers making them more meaningful. This reply still annoys some of these clients, and for a good reason. This type of client has developed an external locust of control, meaning that they believe that their environment controls the way they feel. Some of you may be asking why. Well, if you have an unpredictable childhood, it is easier to give over control entirely than to realize how powerless you are. These clients fail to see their own power, and they deny their own needs. They have become *people pleasers*. Because they come into therapy with the idea that they have no control, this self-fulfilling prophecy sometimes plays out because you cannot come into therapy to try and change others. *You* must try to change yourself. I have gone through months of treatment without certain clients developing this insight. A shame, true, but the thought would hold little value if I introduced it. The client must come to this idea on their own for it to be therapeutically valuable. The very idea goes against the manner in which they have chosen to view the world, so it's an uphill battle. I often hope that the work that we do together will someday kick in, and at times former clients have re-entered treatment when it in fact does. As I have said before, the real work occurs in the clients' environment—not in the therapist's office. As in learning to tie one's shoes, new thought processes require practice to achieve the desired result. It is only human arrogance that makes individuals believe that they have advanced to a higher level of problem solving, when in fact, there is no better way to learn than through repeated practice (even if it's out of a book). There is no magic pill, and no pill will cure panic or anxiety. Pills only mask symptoms, and no pill seems to mask them all.

Commitment

The biggest problem in treating panic disorder is the level of commitment of the client in treatment process. This is not to say that sufferers do not want to get better—of course, they do! However, they are so bewildered and upset from their condition that they often see the condition as hopeless or, in many cases, something they have learned to live with so that they don't seek treatment in the first place. Also, in our busy society, it appears very difficult for people to take the time out to work on something as intangible as anxiety. Instead, some anxiety sufferers make excuses and blame others for their condition. This approach is aggressive in nature and further evidences their belief in an external locus of control. After all, if it's not your fault, you can't be held responsible to fix it—can you?

Choosing a Therapist

For those clients that do seek treatment, they experience a variety of different approaches from the many so-called professionals out there. Many of these "professionals" are weekend warriors, or they practice privately in the evening for some extra cash to supplement some civil service job, some school district job, or such. Treating panic takes a huge commitment on part of the client, and "the professional." The professional should be committed to treating his or her clients on a full-time basis. This is not to say many part-time clinicians are not qualified, but that their availability could limit their effectiveness, their skill level, and their ability to understand your problem fully. Would you go to a surgeon for knee surgery that only practices in the evening, after his/her full-time job in a school district? If nothing else, you have to consider the fatigue factor—they work two jobs—I'm sure you want your therapist to be fully attentive, or else what would be the point?

Most clients choose a therapist based on a referral from a friend, or who has the largest ad in the phone book. The flaw in the first of the proceeding cognitions is that while the therapist may have done well by your friend, he/she may not be right for you! Every person is unique, and your issues may require a different approach. Few graduate schools spend much time on teaching students the "how tos" of treating clients, and it is the *commitment* on the part of the "professional" that dictates their ability to work with particular clients. For example, the nuisances of working with a couple seeking marriage counseling is far different than treating a person with panic. It is for this reason that clinicians should be screened by the client during their first meeting. Most clinicians prefer this as well that way they can better know who is coming to see them and what approach to brandish. First, ask a clinician what their limitations are, as they cannot be effective with all clients; and they should know themselves well enough to answer this question with detail. If they have no limits, move on! If the clinician doesn't know himself/herself, they surely cannot help you. The second thing to ask a clinician is what therapeutic milieu they primarily use in treating clients with panic disorder. If they say anything other than a cognitive-behavioral approach—move on! The cognitive-behavioral approach is the single most effective way of treating people with panic and other anxiety disorders. Anything else is just psycho babble. The treatment of panic disorder requires directed working sessions, and anything else is just fluff that isn't effective in achieving the goal. Third, the client must feel comfortable with the clinician immediately because client-therapist fit is crucial to treatment regardless of the disorder being treated. Don't sit there during a first meeting thinking to yourself, "Well, I'm really not comfortable, but maybe that is how it's supposed to feel; maybe he/she will grow on me." Not happening! If you don't have an initial feeling of comfort, you've just lost forty-five minutes to an hour of treatment time and whatever that person just charged you. No comfort—on to the next! The clinician—client trust level must be very high in treating panic disorder because of the mode of treatment often utilized. Fourth, and lastly, ask how long does the treatment of panic disorder usually take? This is your final indicator in determining if you will be wasting your time and money. I have found that the successful treatment of panic disorder can take anywhere from four months to a year. If you are promised a rose garden, walk away! Everyone is different and nobody, neither you, nor the clinician, can truly tell how long treatment will last. However, you do want to hear the clinician tell you that treatment will end when *you* feel it's appropriate.

Panic disorder is based in the sporadic, irrational thoughts of the client, and it is my experience that these irrational thoughts cannot be overcome alone, because one needs an outside perspective.

Cognitive Restructuring

It is essential that the clinician uses present-day irrational thought patterns; and I'm sure there are plenty, to confront in a therapeutic manner. This confrontation and redirecting is that which I referred to as *cognitive restructuring*. Through this process, the client can begin to learn about themselves to make necessary changes, always in a timely fashion that the client can handle. This is the bulk of the therapeutic work. It builds self-esteem through repeated clinician acknowledgement of client success throughout the therapeutic process and further provides the client with the positive reinforcement to alter their thought patterns as such.

Change in Perspective

Many people who have come to my office in search of a magical cure have been greatly disappointed. Working on panic or anxiety is hard work. Here's how the process works:

1. The clinician provides the structure through which the client does the work.
2. The real "work" occurs outside of the therapist's office by the client.

In essence, the client explores their own environment from the secure base of the therapist's office. The therapist's office becomes a "pseudo holding environment." Overtime, this relationship causes a change in perspective for the client. A perspective in which they remain in the present and remain focused.

The Temporal Component

People suffering from panic and anxiety often appear unfixed in time with regard to their thoughts, considering the past, present, and future simultaneously almost all the time. Whew! Doesn't it wear you out just thinking about it!

Staying in the Present

I work with all of my clients who suffer from panic and anxiety on staying in the present. This is a tremendously difficult concept for them to get right off the bat. The first thing I do in this regard is to establish with them that the past no longer exists. It is merely a shadow of what has been. Many times the client looks at me in disbelief at this moment. I have had many say to me: "What are you crazy? If I could stop thinking about the past I wouldn't need you." And they are all right. But they can't stop without an outside perspective! This process of developing a present-day perspective takes time, and it is quite repetitious in nature. This is accomplished by addressing the client's many present-day relationships with both people and institutions. By using the process of cognitive restructuring, the therapist puts the subject's relationships in a present-day perspective.

www.ingramcontent.com/pod-product-compliance
Lightning Source LLC
Chambersburg PA
CBHW061228280526
45784CB00006B/2685